Then

ALSO BY LINDA BLACK

Inventory
Root
The Son of a Shoemaker
Slant

Linda Black

Then

Shearsman Books

First published in the United Kingdom in 2021 by
Shearsman Books Ltd
PO Box 4239
Swindon
SN3 9FN

Shearsman Books Ltd Registered Office
30–31 St. James Place, Mangotsfield, Bristol BS16 9JB
(this address not for correspondence)

www.shearsman.com

ISBN 978-1-84861-745-2

Copyright © Linda Black, 2021.
The right of Linda Black to be identified as the author of this work has been asserted by her in accordance with the Copyrights, Designs and Patents Act of 1988. All rights reserved.

ACKNOWLEDGEMENTS
My heartfelt thanks to Claire Crowther and Mimi Khalvati
for their support and their insights, and of course to Tony Frazer.

Thank you to the Editors of the following journals in which some of these poems have previously appeared: *Blackbox Manifold, Envoi, Fortnightly Review, Molly Bloom, Poetry Wales, Perverse, Scintilla, Stand* and *Prototype 2 Anthology.*

'Time' was a prize winner in the 2012
Ledbury Poetry Festival Competition judged by Ian Duhig.

The final poem, 'Cento: In my vignettes', was sourced from poems published in *Long Poem Magazine* Issue 14, Autumn 2015
http://longpoemmagazine.org.uk/issues/issue-fourteen/

Contents

TIME
Time is of the effervescence	11
There were bolts	12
Referencing the house	13
Into the haystack	14
Missing the route	15
Plosive	16
I found you	17
Summative	18

MISDEMEANOUR
Misdemeanour	21
Here	22
The bones in his legs	23
His lame legs	23
'He lay down'	24
I pick out	24
A pen a trace	25
Mother	26
I speak to thee…	27
A white cup	28
Bless you for you are gone	29
I like	29

FRIPPARY
Frippary	33
Much sequencing	34
Here and there	34
There are folds	35
Rails of dresses	35
Girl in peril	36
It opened into a sort of….	37
What she is wearing today she may not have	38
Wake	40
Her clothes worked well	41

The un-envisaged

The un-envisaged	45
A smidgen	46
Chastise	48
Kitchen	48
Bagatelle	49
Break down	50
A wooded head	50
A man chewing a bone	50
Clue	51
Pale days	51
Too many holes	51
Scholar	52
Limpet/id	53
PeOpLe/d _ _ _ _ _ _ _ _ _ _	54
Breed	55
Staple together	56

If I were to calculate

If I were to calculate	59
The boy is getting too many for me…	60
In the sense	61
'Terrability'	62
Full grown	63
Sorrow fallow harrow	64
A henchman	65
Explosion / exclusion	66
The thrum string strain	67
To bed with wishes and hopes	68

Riddle

Riddle	71
Ware	72
Topic	73
Scatterbox	73
A small misfortune	75
Skittles & Pigs	76

Scarper

Scarper	79
Converse	80
Capable of flux	80
Cuttings	81
Correct	81
Vignettes	82
Extreme conditions	82
In the articled world	83
Pick the lock	83
A gully	84
I was alone with the child	85

Each shell or barnacle

Each shell or barnacle	89
Come side with me	90
Prompt	90
My goal	91
Trills	91
I have folded	91
With the garden	92
I poach my meanings	92
Haul	93
Here is tin	93
All she could see were their eyes	94
Rag bag	94
Rows	95
Words	96
Lark	97
A Causeway Runneling…	98

Afterword

Cento: In my vignettes	103

Time…

Time is of the effervescence

Then it's popped. Likewise a pillar of well-being – too much taboo contravenes the notion all's well. Many are non-believers confounding the desire to know. An expansive watch tells it all.

It isn't over yet. The addition of qualifiers proves it. Print more than one copy; copy more than one print, then you have an edition, each an original so to speak. Signature consumes time. The stress she is wearing does not come off in the wash nor fall discarded to the bathroom floor.

Tolerate the unknown, the intimation. In turn are the hours. Parameters reach outward. The twang of elastic nullifies the outcome. Come out and play pity. A visit to the cinema can be a panacea.

The rule comes free inside the cracker. Coils in hand. Trifle is lighter on the stomach. This is the wider palate, though succinct. A dichotomy requires lunch like any other – the menu only guessed at. Press the space bar. Separate meat and milk as did some forefathers (hers anyway).

Measure/s for safe keeping. A hand's spic and span, a table's spoon. Tawdry by definition, a second hands back what cannot be divvied up. Stay still why don't you! Epic!

On the dot. Safety behind the door. Larger than the frame it purports to fit. Come winter down it goes – contradicted and back to size. A swell beginning for a venture.

There were bolts

on the floor   splinters
struck in spite   &   then
I began   bordered   to
inattention   doused
in jelly   sweet & clear
wrapped in a dish cloth   *ikle trickle monkey*
albumen   ring of worms   bites
to the ear   pickled
egg   bit
of a tear

And then I began
on the floor   from the floor
through the hatch
preserve & persevere   bits
of hair   fuzzy
veneer   finger wax
pea   plea
piddle-de-dee

Referencing the house

Constant
declarations of intent   posthumous
gatherings seeking
tension   a foot-stool
to reach the latch   trap-
door   bereft of sentry
regularities charities   the birth
of a cinder   salt   malt
cellular activity
nipples undergarments
smatter of fat   stock
supply / supplies   a lick   *splat clip spit chap*
something   needs
moving   *proving   chewing   screwing*

Into the haystack

A large pile built up. The launderette lay around the corner. In the window a surfeit of powder. A welcome of sorts.

Before (she) was longed for that was the way it went. An appointment was made to last. Left hand tied behind the back.

Chalk and taupe. The colour of mole. Ringworm, scabies, dermatitis, pox. Layette. Various combinations. Long John ran six feet. Was that where the treasure was?

Got the bone needle? An eye for a hook? Objects resemble. Look afield. Look again. Fodder in the loft. Conical, ridged on top, built for preservation.

The needle was carefully hidden by museum director Jean de Loisy, at the Palais de Tokyo contemporary art gallery in the French capital. Sven Sachsalber spent the next two days trying to find it.

Ouch!

Missing the route

Seconded
to another family   gate
secured   *latch . . . clatch*
bloodletting   improper play   *ping . . . dismay*
collude / allude   right
old racket   ring
fenced   unsightly   frisked   slightly
sick   drabs / pacts / defecation
infestation − something
beginning with … *m /s / pe*
cul-de-sac   an extra tray
of victuals   virals   vitals (overfed)
for commiseration   gratification / subjugation
Denial   worm-holes   defects
genitalia   (in a practical way)
diffidence   delay   a ray   (x-ray -rating)
of escape   confrontation   dis-
combobulation
Sniff the daisies   often
overblown

Plosive

Routines make the way clearer. Follow the one in uniform. Spit into this. Put your feet up. At 36 weeks he bursts out.

Personalised disorder in private, not some flimsy curtain unfit for purpose. You should see the insides!

Long kitchens can be useful for folding sheets. Plenty other palaver.

Family implodes. Occludes the vocal tract, stopping the airflow. Were we ghosts or surrogates roaming the streets eyes cut out?

Pangs. Spasms. Lucozade. *Pop!* the weasel goes (a scornful riposte * *see note*). From the glottis to the lips. A sudden release. Not quiet like this.

The soft palette reconvenes, articulate, velar. Consonants raised towards the velum – *rat-pat, tit-tat, bit-kin, pith-bin, bad-pin.* Save the misery tin. Stoke it up.

---

* '…Sergeant Smith apprehended Huxtable at Williams's house, and told him what he was charged with, namely, stealing the plate … to which he only replied, "Pop goes the weasel." *The Times* (London, England), 5 July 1853, p. 7: Middlesex Sessions, July 4'

I found you

floating between windpipe
& epiglottis scum
on your lips *lump bump*
little hump ingrained
toenail ungrateful
persona attempts at misery
unconstrained , , , dental needs false
recollection *test me call me*
out a clever guise long brown
testament scallywag
dissenter

Summative

Something shakes the infirm – an ailment within. Let's leave it there. What has been said? In its base form aggregate reminds of tar on the wayside – an instant childish drop back. Flint in the mudflats, and in the sand (Skegness) a hole filled with sea.

Taken as a whole, tea with sugar reminds of dishwater, which was how it tasted she said (due to the esteem in which *that* particular brewer was held). Sources unite in what may be believed. In law the impossibility of the lay mind may be seen as a jest. Funny this business couched in wig and gown, with all due respect to the unexpected outcome.

Everyone likes to laugh in admiration of mirth, in place of community. When I was a kid, people used to cover me with cream and put cherries on my head. It was tough in the gateau. (Acknowledgements due.)

Back inside the component parts something concretes. A wobbly experience this growing up thing. In-laws notice first commenting on the sofa, cups and saucers wavering through the hatch. Choose your construct. Usually coconut pyramids on a backdrop of doily.

Arguments count – inflections court misery, soon to be realised. The colour that surrounds can charm (brocade) or lead to dysfunction (gate-leg table). Thoughts to work on (bric-à-brac). We must look up to something. Finally said, it all adds up to much.

Misdemeanour…

Misdemeanour

For the life of me. Accordingly fixated apropos an earlier thought. The bell dangles. At which there dingles. Insufficient evidence, not for want of error.

Breadcrumbs, ants on the surface. One can feel sorry, as with slugs. Which takes me to the garden. Tidying up is the bane to chivvying on. Things to prepare. A little basket atop the dresser. Put upon. A jar of wasps on the window ledge. Jammy buggers.

Takes away. Old Park Road, Ingledew Crescent, blue moon. Suppose the dolls' home came to good use round the children's home. I searched for it in the Hayward – little lights in empty rooms, some in total darkness. Everyone was out.

Little makes for sentiment and what's wrong with that? Came tumbling down. Friar Tuck and all that. Have you ever had a conversation about mangles? What fun they were.

I arrange it all, counting back. Handstands were for others. Blood might rush to my head. Would you put Smarties in a pewter bowl and leave them lying around saying *eat me* in different hues, all chattering at once, and then chastise? Of course not.

So, what's on telly? Forget it, I didn't really mean. Several jigsaw puzzles are waiting to be done.

Here

Was as a deteriorating moment, defined and out of the way. Breakfast, whatever the situation . Mood bored. We live like this, decipher. Outside, the Amelanchier sweetly blooms.

What should be said? Moulding, mouldering. Lost joy, a stolen cameo ring. Collaborate with past intentions.

Sieved, the little holes adequate, nor unexpected. The sink is cracked, the crack spreading. Disparate fissures conjoin.

Define slippers, step careful. Callipers may bear the weight of a father, his withered leg. Pilchards or anchovies? Meaning peeled of intent.

A basement is halfway between. Coal below, the purpose consumed. Sun combined with frost may alter consciousness, as too the carrion crow.

This is the season of black spot, lighter evenings, when the body may slough its skin.

Shadbush, shadwood or shadblow, serviceberry or sarvisberry, or just sarvis; juneberry, saskatoon, sugarplum or wild-plum, chuckley pear.

The bones in his legs

shone   thin   as a half carrot
his stick walking   pinched
a crooked inch   mashed marrow
piss slaver snore
I could not save him

His lame legs

       held him
encased him   deceived him
deluded him   a stick
felled him   feebled him   held him
slack   flak   bamboozled him
wasted him   hoovered him
his bones entombed him   mind
eluded him   her mind
slapped him   wrapped him
concluded him   his lame legs
defined him   and his life
wore wrong

'He lay down'

I read   and an image comes – not of him
my father   but a dormant parasol
beached on the verandah   its skirts
declined limp   all life
gone out of them   – he lay down
his aim   his snow-covered
memory   his latent humility
his spent head   and alone
was he and remaindered

I pick out

Her flab & varnish   Her arm & a leg
His aquiline nose   His twisted gait
His collared bone   His drab & his dibble
I find out   Her swipe & slate
Their seldom fate   *I duck out*
I slide out   *They slip away*

A pen a trace

of dissent   count back
to where a feather
may come from   a slip
of the wrist   a beckoning
you can't quite see — a snarl a loop
a trick of the senses   a father
in a dapper suit plaid fabric
wide lapels pocket handkerchief
come night his polished shoes
wade through mud   his heart
in my head / hand
his turned down face

Mother

with the perfect
script mother   mother
with the matching
sleeves   quite comfortable
off mother fed
to the teeth   swollen
mother slid
from grace   (un) well
combed mother
with the made up eyes
flat iron mother
about faced   mother
dead mother

I speak to thee…

Thee with fine assumptions
in folds across the land   attuned
to intricate longings

How would I approach thee?

Discreet are the traces
no visible means   no other's   landscape
gives surety   on which
to tread   lightly

I may never see

The sun on your mantle
your shelves   laden
with afterthought   lacking   a pin
to hold thee

I yearn for consideration

A makeshift engagement   which may be
partition   your little window
shrinking   having   promised
nothing   and all
that nothing   is

I shall gift thee

A swarm of marigolds
a past   item
tenderly

A white cup

A closed handle a row of glass dishes
on an uppermost shelf
a crack in a window-pane

To consider the periphery
the meniscus still
as a frozen lake

A paint-scuffed chair
a fringe of discomfort thrift
of the meanest kind

Involvement at any given moment
a habit sly
and ever drifting

A teaspoon a napkin a silvered bowl
light on the borderline
just passing through

Bless you for you are gone

and I have no religion
you are driving an unroadworthy car
you are painting the hallway
black the ceiling too we return
years later to retrieve the lampshade
– an upturned glass tulip pink
and terminal you would
have been a Tolpuddle Martyr
rolled up your sleeves
and entered any fray

I like

to close the door
and to sit in the corner
if it was up to me
I'd deem you well
alive and well
and sitting opposite

Frippery…

Frippery

Pull out the safety net attributed to the defence of the realm. Flatten for ironing – bibs, rags, antimacassar. Unimportant considerations. Turpentine. Formica. An extra leaf (dropped). Dumb waiter.

Stays at home. Self-binding. An inverted cone shape. So many bundles. A jar for everything except the kitchen sink. Everyone accepts the kitchen sink.

Gaudy. With matching cuff-links. (Just the ticket for a strapless gala.) Worn on the abdomen. Stiffened with glue. A brow raised. A broken rib.

They had but little clothing, but such as they had was fanciful in character and fantastic in its arrangement. Any little absurd gewgaw or gimcrack they had they disposed in such a way as to make it attract attention most readily.

Ardass, arrasene, balzarine, bedraggled; bombazine, bagging, barathea, course and stout. Cap it all. Make it up. (That flower pot shape is very smart.)

Much sequencing

with the odd pulled accord
cardigans left hanging
for each age   appliquéd
fair isle fair trade double
crossed simply plied   containers
for the family remembrances
of pain or glory
the passing years

Here and there

arms are woven   multiple
underwear   sleeves and pockets
unfulfilled   carriage
and posture   an itch to the ear
accoutrements   hitched
on the back   internal organs
all wrapped up   a cuticle
a critical heel   the well-made
face   many wear hats
simultaneous coats exeunt
in small steps

There are folds

to examine – creases
imbedded   tacking
is evenly placed
do I need to measure
accuracy

Rails of dresses

hem-locked wind-blown
true dress skew dress a scantling
of hope lattice wear   waisted
unbuttoned gathered
and primed – the colour
of brass worn in a field
side-swept a hand
holding a hat
ribbons   flaying

Girl in peril

A floored penny, a floundering fluke, on a hillside, in a headscarf, about to depart. Scoots back her chair a short distance. Closes the table. Fills a thermos with salt. Throws it in a particular direction.

An orphan, a scallywag, the bane of her (own) life, speeds across a frozen lake. Rides side-saddle, handlebars, dobbins (often found in children's tales). Clip-clop, gob-stop, trip-trap, fan and gander.

In a pantomime, a ballet, a spic and a span : old tricks, bold tricks, up the ginnel. A tomboy, a minx, a problem on the page. Devilish (with pigtails). In *black and red apparel,* The faces she pulls!

General girl, girl for all seasons. A skater, a skelter, negotiating rapids, leaping over hurdles, standing on her head – guide-girl, toffee-tyke, pip in a pen. Rescuing the doctor, fetching the dog. In a hissy-fit; pinned on the lid of a tin.

It opened into a sort of....
(*Little Jewel*, Patrick Modiano)

O<small>nto</small> ,,,   the page turns ... woman
in a yellow coat   will she be
anticipated?   ½ yes ½ no

V<small>ariation</small> ,,,   *past the brick apartment block*
small sack of space   flattered field
exposed branch   dip ending
en clave / closure / trance

T<small>urn</small> ,,,   *reduced the distance between us*
reservoir heap   wearing
(this woman) slipper socks   a
carved face

M<small>arker</small> ,,,   *with the gait of a dancer*
more of a mourning   relief
after all that murder

A motherless life

What she is wearing today she may not have

Moreover the hindrance, in terms of matching or modified. Suppose it is done and frequent as the moth. The doomed fly dies in the corner swept and located. All this before breakfast. Explicit in his nature the rag and bone man came and went under the arches.

Slipped on the shoe. Many laced and pin-tucked as featured. Browse for the time being. Snag a caught loop on a chain. There are many ways to travail for example on the slide without a care. Never having driven nor for that matter the length of a thread. Forewarned is to dangle, toes tapping.

Specifically the description means blue with its many connotations. Having set that in the store room a stool begs for velvet, mistakes the length it may go to. Bulbous those ankles with the stockings down. Back in the sack. A week minus five percent, that's fortune eyes down.

Now for the starter. Statistically it's a no-brainer. Bra and pants to match. On the way to the kitchen forever and always. Pre reassembly. The catalogue is back with many to choose from on your day off.

Before you know it, it needs washing again and not without questions. As too is the haircut. The letter writer writes that's what they do. Not always at the same pace. Today the sheet changes, latterly unaccounted for in bold configurations, also anticipation. The same old trousers pull quietly on.

Circles, triangles and oblongs especially rearranged. If you think this quiet! Simple though calls for concentration. If you think this simple! Hanging out is a must when the wind blows. As of this morning, marking distances and breaking things. Arms bruise easily and there's the reminder.

As it is another day. With some relief on the outfit at the outset. The key is in the colour more or less. Adhering to the view that toenails and fingernails need not match, the street is marginally the same. That come and go business.

What seems to be the problem? Is it in the manufacture. Mother knew best. It was all in the folded. Piles on the floor laundered in the most perceptive way. If only parents weren't so bothered. Concurrently childbirth is all hot water – or at least warm.

Popeye liked spinach. It was as if everyone else knew. There's a film called *Sliding Doors*. Also *Groundhog Day*. The point is called the domino effect. Or how the things that may not have been may have been if you walked a different way. This isn't in the end.

Wake

I have dressed
well enough – straps   dashes   a series
of uncollected   fizz
and fizzle out

Her clothes worked well

– stippled vest, ingrained elastic, nurtured bodice, the stent of a full demeanour. A staged game – *her* game. All roads crossed by nature, stalled by lights expending motes. Control, dingbats of caution.

In her were words of difference. Nicked, notched, snatched. She'd carried on. Threadbare. No bike to get on. Simultaneously through school and puberty. Imagine a dead hedgehog. Imagine her bleeding shame. Racemes of it.

The bleeding-heart dove is shy and secretive. The bleeding-heart dove (genus *Gallicolumba*) has a pronounced reddish hue extending down the belly.

Char char charcoal – bolts & burns, briars & barnacles. A/bashed. In the snick of the woods, the pike of the lane (predatory with large teeth), the skew of the ginnel, yaw of the byway.

Spittle and grimace. The illusion of blood: post-box, signal-box, fire-engine, guts. No back up, no back-drop, no back-chat *–bone –stab –slap –lash –bite –hand –story*. Blackout.

The un-envisaged…

The un-envisaged

Slow down, look up. Ten people (inside/out) at any time may change. Is half an hour long enough? Time to make stock. An uninformed informal guest. A mouse under the fridge.

To summarise: minute railings, pepper cravings, carved brass, splosh-splash, daily flailing, cost of ailing, swollen handles, beer & candles, skin & simmer, what's for dinner (pie & mush, bowl of slush).

A smidgen

        Of fudge   a...
scr*ea*m of carrion   f*a*t-lipped   drained
     of FANCY   a st*o*rm
in a st*o*mach   walls   str-*e-e-e*-tch
      churn reg*urg*it*ate*   just a   little
  bit MORE   salvation : latkes   tzimmus
lokshen-kugel – rugelach   kneidlach   eingemachts
   fish-cakes &   chrain   a sliver   of liver
    salts
      EYES tooo *big*... plate piled

over the limit   SUCCUMB   *suck suck succour*
      to greed &   habit Se*rr*ated lip
T*e*mpered tongue SOUL
     dis*tend*ed   mandible   *tripe gutter-snipe*

deep veined
   conflict
     B*r*ing me
a morsel   an emptied   shell   a
    wished-bone   WHITE meat
       cooked-out   *de-jug   chewed-cud*
F*e*ed me   pea-pudding   *gib*lets   dripping
                        g
   s*mash*ed   BLUBBER   g
T*e*nder heart!   S*u*rrogate!   Sav(i)our!

>   scales
> STICK   in the g*ull*et   a   fork
>   is a powerful tool
>   I des*ire*
> a bowl of cake   a broth   *hot-pot gob-stop*
>   of scalded chicken   a cut-glass
> reservoir   DON'T serve me
>   Octopus   *de*prived
> of its m*ate*   Lay gall-stones
>   around my pl*ate*

Chastise

Tell me off, bone-hook, slacker. I am minded, acute, grizzly, disinfected. Synch your earlobes. Persecute. Give yourself breakfast. Fuss over remains. Dart well about. *Nail & Bracket, Pail & Slaughter.* Drink up I tell you, I am dizzy! A pit, a hullabaloo. Do unto you as I am bid. My head in your hands. *Pot, kettle.*

Kitchen

sinks   store room

steadfast

daily bred   after words

the clearing up

Bagatelle

Bilious little bugger: belly up, head banged, bounced off the stairwell (don't tell, home is hell). Filigree mouldings, obscured passageway, spotted glass – regular little nipples.

Pock holes: porridge unattended. Pogged (Yorkshire) at the table. Insufficient marrow. Dissed backbone. Metal health. Balls: Up (set at 9 in the 19th century). Guarded by wooden pegs: penalties, obstacles – laterally related to golf. Ricocheted off pins.

Sticks: cue, yard, pogo, pretzel, giving it (singular). When used as a unit, usually 2 inches (5.08cm in the international inch). 18–36 inches (460–910 mm) long, with a fluted handle. Diversion: primary target, large nerve clusters (the common peroneal in the mid-thigh). Only the tip strikes.

Break down

in a stair well   a stuck lift
when there is kindness
a solid spoon   on the carbon field
of a grandmother's carpet
after dissolution
in a Spanish lesson   why not
a basement room

A wooded head

crow cawing   fly
crawling   soul
mistake a growl
in the making   shakes
skin flakes

A man chewing a bone

does not seem
natural – its length
akin to a forearm – picked
clean   the dead
scream to me

Clue

in a single cup / line / fold
an insect crawls –
complex   bleak all over
more shocked   than betwixt
sharpness   may be named
obscure   as it is flung
so   may it reap

Pale days

supplication   I made
I tumbled   I dis-em-bo-died
daughter!   daughter!
would you not think
by now   by whom

Too many holes

spoil the surface   regularity
pointed   inbred   staged
for discomfort   the slide
down the spine   runaway versions
of over and over   pot holes
pox holes   O O O

Scholar

Magnifies, stretches the point, lengthens out and up. Critical blinking, conspicuous minor errors. Quibbling pedant. Does such and such end in double l? The case rests, lowered. Seasoned doubt, fabrication.

Chair can be defined, and Trypophobia – from *the primitive portion of the brain*. Lotus seeds may trigger repulsion.

Own it all. Create a fount, a bibliography. Students would agree, agreeably side-tricked.

Limpet/id

Debris
- Melanoma
- Misnomer
- Metasoma
- Nom-de-plume

A game of quibble dabble dribble   scree flee return to jail
pet pet pet   pit pat poke
Props   cake-tin   throne
Homemade theatre
Gretel (regret all)
Pinocchio
Mr Turnip
Scorn forlorn   groan moan   dropped scone
defiled reviled
Sentence   subjugation
Pincers   ointment   medication
Plastic sheet   heart bleat

PeOpLe/d _ _ _ _ _ _ _ _ _ _

Dull & Or/derly   Cell-Contained

Mis (in) formed   Desolate   Dis-Junked

Parquet-Floored   Call-Centred   De-

Selected   Blub & Dribble   Drip & Dabble

Trouble-Bent   Low & Saddled   Flat & Spent

Squint   Skint-Flint   Mash   Double-Crass

Kippers   Fluffy Slippers   Shelf-Life

Thickly-Battered   Boned

Alive   Glass-Slug   Chewed-Cud

Breed

Imprint, thumbnail – part of a cat (retractile claws), a missed event*, nestlings, capers, feathered scraps.

Noisy miners (multiple broods), netted spoils, quaint minimal Fletchlings (with reddish-orange heads and a triangular yellow mark on the back of each eye).

Trained hangers (on) selected robes, sizes prone to incretion. Coats and arms; hereditary saturation.

Step away till later. Corrected drafts (keg or cask). Mannerisms are a balanced book. Scour of *dip-THEER-ee-uh*. Sentence, sustenance, ail-a-men-tary canal.

Temporary spots. Incompleted complications. Fences, former inferences. Splints, braces, (a) coddled cheek.

---

* I had the chance to control several Pelham puppets.

Staple together

Wiseacre   I challenge you
traitor   executor   *trip-tape   tricker-trap*
trading   in
artefact – gesticulation

Scathe & slander
slake & simmer   sell me
a soupçon
of misconception   a mess
of adhesive

Go savour   go image   go train yourself
to flounder   *flannel-fish   fluke-eye   mizzle-pan   clam*
in a soup   a middling broth
of make-believe

If I were to calculate…

If I were to calculate

(An anathema to me) the number of slights (I have) placed upon my own shoulders, what benefit? Who knows, let alone that self that may be me?

Prior knowledge clots the reservoir – wasted matter disintegrates: slumps of fat. Basted moment/s. Take/s the time. Close the door on tedium. Procrastinate – create (a) tension (graph). On a scale from 1 to 10. Many mortals feel the same.

For a small fee a record/ing may be made. Pronounce/d metaphysical – investigate. Any answers? Your view matters, however unpalatable.

The boy is getting too many for me said Mr Cruncher...
(*A Tale of Two Cities*, Dickens)

I had seen him before with his dimly lit eyes, his incalcitrant lip, his sweat and bones. Too little, too leaning. Though I admit to liking that in a wall or the trunk of a tree. Don't think I am harshly inclined.

I had heard his mood his malefaction his slight tenancy of mind, tasted the fruit of his carapace. Sweetly I dazed upon him, framed his face in the ovaries of his eyes. He needed a benefactor, but maybe so did I. Don't think I complain.

I had seen him skip, reading the last page first. When I snorted he would not retort. He had read many an ending, for that was his concern. Apparently he'd been brought up that way, with many ways to predict; his future but one. Please don't imagine I am credulous.

I heard his wimp, his whine and snarl, his sneer and the occasional giggle. He could play the trumpet, while I could only figure. I added his plusses and minuses, condemned his indifference then subtracted. Don't wonder at my disparity.

I saw what I wanted, for which I am not proud. Each prolonged stare became only a stump in an ever changing stratosphere. His socks were always dirty white. Do not think I snub.

I saved up my pennies, bought him drainpipes to share goodwill. They sparkled like disintegrated diamonds. I played tiddlywinks, jacks, pin the tail, but not with him. I saw him scrutinise the flick of my thumb, my ping-pong retaliation. I hid him but he still peered through me. Every whichaway, ubiquitous like Wally, a pale flame like Will o' the Wisp.

In the sense

of skulduggery   a rich
reward   a clip to the ear
the egg   is broken   turned
whipped   exasperated
a fellow traveller
beats the track – fellow traveller
under the skin   pocket me   bowl
me over   a pale grey day   the colour
of death   I hold   a certificate
in contemplation   – the coming
– a lone   meander – terms
of my contract

'Terrability'
(James Joyce, *Ulysses*)

Scrape of day   strapped
for cash   raw-boned   drained
of expectancy   Light
disobeys   greys   the skin
infused   with lament   drags
excuses   under   the floor
Torpor Taxidermy   (enter
a rodent) a fillet of pity   soon
to be scarified   *strip / strop / impair
trip / trap / tear*   rent
arrear   conclude   &   calcify
finickity finality   extent
of mortality

Full grown

Cavities centrality stature – tree
wavers sings / swings / bows
is maze entanglement
solidarity Overseer (up-thrust)
whispers sways Circularity
poise shade protection (eggs/the odd owl)
hollow-bellied disparate
egalitarian Occasional
prosperity (acorn/fruit)
rigidity incision
disability deformity irregularity
tragedy From which
a rope may be strung

Sorrow fallow harrow

I read about a hawk
– how to kill
bite & swallow O
lesser beings! rabbits jackdaws mice
skinned alive *trip-trap*
the crooked bridge sparrow
& pheasant the collapse
of a colony *–coo–coo –co–co*
coop coop lowly
creatures *M*arrow
*S*orrow *F*allow *H*allow

A henchman

trails the stairs   pocketsful
of jewels smut
on the walls   house
ricochets   treads
dark weather   shadow
serpent under the bed
nick-pick *grab grab grab*
pinch half-inch
down the well
rat tat tat

Explosion / exclusion

Whelp and whippet, scald and kerosene A blind lamp qualified for blunder. Do you see? Exposure, a dirt bed – the end of the prowling season. Unpalatable, ungroomed. Grime and shufty. On the way through the woods sharpened by the breeze, squeeze, creed, need. Forget-me-not, quince and spider (I am your friend – look after me). The rush across the stones – tip-toe, moon-flit, coal-lit, belongs nowhere. Heel, steal, holes in the pocket/socks. Pick it up, slay, throw it away. Think of the morrow. Seclusion, intrusion. All in the head.

The thrum string strain

Of suggestion   each
persisting – *thrum*
combines with   ring   or hum   or bell
or inner defeat   – buzz
off why don't you

String mocks the singular   forms
a cavalcade   a carousel
bangs on   on   on

Strain offers a bargain
demonstrates
how   not   off course
calamity   can be
or foreboding

Call my refrain   a form
of recitation ……. my favourite
polyphony

To bed with wishes and hopes

Propped head   scalded factory
a scythe a sickle a swathe
crick / spasm / pang   continue
the loop lip-synced   beleaguered
immured ... *I listened*
but was not taught   a waste
of inclination sample
illusions (cane/walking-frame)
contusions   buffeted   intuit
have you ever ...

Riddle…

Riddle

Head fold   arm swivel   *twizzle drizzle*
polarised eyes   meagre penniless
concave gaze   a turn   a tail   *slight flea-bite*
foot drop   (under the arches   second left)
stiff back/ed linen   hump lump   impeded gait
older days   leaden light   adult daze
paralysis   (atypical depression)
quarried tiles (misfit)   *slab slap overlap*
assemblage of nuts & bolts   (hard wear)
crockery mockery (Scott not free)
calories count   stark Clark's shoes
spleen   Scalextric running late

Ware

Enid Seeney (b.1931 d.2011) drew kidney-shaped coffee-tables, Fifties sideboards, easy-chairs: Day's recliner, Bernadotte's sofa. Domestic objects fair flew across the plates. Everyday pottery makes a home. *Mason's* cracks easily for all its wealth.

A 'muffin-maker' makes plates, 4/500 in a day (generally about 320) no more than 7 ins in diameter. Is it necessary to explain? Concerning cutlery were canteens. Spoons not to be confused. Fish-knives, sugar-tongs. Crumb trails. Liberated mould. The road forks. Where o ware! Oven and earth. Takes the same type of biscuit.

Eric Gill (b.1882 d.1940) left Ditchling Village for Hopkins Crank; 'an unreconstructed Georgian squatter's cottage.' Home-killed pig, home-baked bread. *All be in the soup together.* Animalistic variations: the cow of a jug, funnel-mouth, hind-parts hidden. Big belly spouting. Relative cosiness. Preliminary to something less uncommon. *Neither the schools nor society had tinctured his strong nature.*

Silicosis 'chronic simple' – miner's phthisis, grinder's asthma, potter's rot (can become complicated). Running in all weathers. Considerably heated (130 º F). Little legs breathing in. *At the age of seven, his education being complete, he was summoned into the world ... Darius was first taken to work by his mother. It was the winter of 1835, January ...* (J. B. Davis, Surgeon c.1840).

Did you know George Formby (b.1904 d.1961) held the world premiere of his first sound film, *Boots! Boots!* in Burslem in 1934? (nasal, high-pitched.) Tea-Pot *(15/-)* Mourning cups *(2/6) Two tumblers, and a custard-cup* without a handle. Parian and porcelain, whiteware and luster. The blackened town hall.

…like a dark Pleiades in a green and empty sky… Handbridge has the shape of a horse and its rider, Bursley of a half donkey, Knype of a pair of trousers, Longshaw of an octopus, and little Turnhill of a beetle. The floors were often thick with wasted clay.

Hannah Barlow (b.1861 d.1916) kept a menagerie. An expert tube liner despite losing the use of her right hand. Women threw since ancient times. Seldom brought to light. Limited (look at Jane Eyre), fainting – ribs removed. Paintress, redress. Hour glass – not accidental. 75-pound bags of clay. Spontaneous abortion.

Faience, impasto, marqueterie, Carrara. '*Doulton Lambeth Large Stoneware Tyg*, sgrafitto – decorated with leaping and grazing deer. Impressed back-stamp, dated to 1876. In v good condition – no chips cracks, hairlines or restoration £850: *Pair Of Royal Doulton Lambeth Hannah Barlow Goats & Children Vases c1900* £1,320.00.' Buy it now, or make an offer. Other artists' work has floundered and died.

Mason & Co. Knight & Elkin. Floyd and Savage. J. W. Pratt. Colclough. Booth. Riddle & Lightfoot. Minton & Boyle. Ginder & Co. W. Ridgeway. Dimmock &Smith. Copstick, jun. Copstick, sen. Bridgewood. Meakin. Wedgwood & Sons: Jiggers, Mould-runners, Oven-boys, Dipper's-boys, Cutters, Handlers, Apprentice Painters, Figure Makers: boys & girls between the ages of 7 & 18, average weekly 2s. 0½d.

Topic

held by elastic – *ping*
tied to a stake   trodden in
meaning   centrefold
leading both ways   greet
the subject
in search of a jester

Scatterbox

Gall-brain | bad-hat | tin-wink | drifter |
Slap-cat | clean-mat | pin-brain | cluster |
Coal-case | nut-face | twin-track | blister |
Pit-break | sea-flake | clout-shine | sister |
Hot-cross | split-pea | flit-flop | twister |
Silly-nilly | hot & chilly |
Distinctly dusted | doused in custard |

A small misfortune

A rag of misapprehension, as a doll may be. I felt little. Akin to misinterpretation. Or was it a broken pen?

What was the message? I thought for myself, and to and of, and did not run awry. I made the assumption, certain as a cleft in a sentence. Vertical and of no volition.

A large puddle lay ahead, fainter than anticipation. The golden retrieval – the chance of salvation. It was I who picked my brains.

The weather began to flag. My soles worn to their utmost. An ancient dilemma. As though the dark were made of ash, or rowan. A canopy for occasions.

It was me I knew , , , It was me , , , It was me again

I bade myself goodnight.

Skittles & Pigs

Ribbed pole	Three-bellied hat	Stripes & clots
Diorama	Fish & figs	Bowl & spindle
Mucker sucker	Bib & tucker	Full-ground
Fair-grind	Pocket sock-it	Davy Crockett
Eff & blind	Spit & swindle	Let-fly bull-pie
Borage porridge	Swill & forage	Pickled rat
Newt & gnat	Hind quarter	Didnae oughta
Strip strap strut	Pick pock pluck	Oopsy dropsy
Out	Of	Luck

Scarper…

Scarper

Before I bag you. Formerly there were places to hide – cabins, balaclavas, mine-shafts, blankets. States of retribution. I ran away, came back, held my own hand. Drought slipped through my fingernails. I and they had to grow.

One single thing is impossible. A saucer, a quart of curdled milk (too true); mashed potato (just the one).

Significant suppers. The road torched. Scram, head for the hills. However one tried. Russian Vine. A rhyme for forgot. Make yourself scarce.

Personality peers. Bumps, lumps, traits… given to me. Lips of balm, Sellotape, unrequited gratitude.

Remove the skin and innards. Stuff the neck. Before proceeding check the weathervane – are the neighbours arguing/making amends?

Blot squat begot; swat plot snot; dry-rot mug-shot; job-lot liver-spot pain-pot; knot slot blud-clot Scapa Flow (go) skedaddle The burglars legged it before the police showed up. The ship leaves at midnight.

Converse

with … goes (on) like
common ground work
exploits *blah blah* the differential
shall we have toast
or batter and how much
longer another mouthful
blood is out of place thicker …
not to worry hurry pure
diversion time to retire
desire (a) p *ie/ea* ce of (my) mind
… than water left/right
brain's desultory ways
the same company

Capable of flux

less of accord remotely
controlled as on a vast plain
some very distance away
where the terrified partly live
pursued by the need
to belong

Cuttings

strewn on the path (put away)
moss insidiously plying
– livid in its green   cringe
at its slow crawl
up the spine   scrape away
 – any implement
will do – a tidy mind
calumnious – tight
in its habit

Correct

the stance   the outward
foot   the assumption
of waking   relish alignment   – a grace
in/animate relations   possessions
whittle them down   – stains tears
minor figurines – selected
pieces of severance

Vignettes

(honour the small occasion)
 – a passive glide
various species of bees (landscape)
sea horses (portrait) floating   static
e – lec – tri – ci – ty (no catalogue): body
– lifeless prone
sparks flashes small explosions
wheels & fires trepidation
streaks incandescence
– bursts & splutters
hinged head raised
from his hospital bed…

Extreme conditions

messages ignored   the faithful
long gone   the walls
distressed   needles & cones
pined for   a carriage clock
rollicking away   heed
contamination   tremble
at such misconception

In the articled world

I look to extraction   humbly
I pine   make use
of dead wood   ends
& snippets   spin my forebears
into fables   take
incomprehensible turns   as senseless
as last night's blunders

Pick the lock

A pointy implement   aligns
in discomfort little triggers
catch & release   make
mince-meal of regulation
– prickling – testy
if I were they would
I let me alone

A gully

Fallen open. Tall intention spread around tall rooms. Sections staged as compromise. Contraindication.

A twisted paradox. Mock plates. Perforated cups. It was breaking time in the staffroom. I was getting a cup of tea. Bags of *colleagues*. This and that has no uniformity. I'm fine I said.

Search for a creed. Glue it down in long thin strips like fly paper. It takes courage to step into the wide boulevard. Consciousness rails against dispersal. One expects trees.

It was breeding time in the auditorium. Not seen to be heard. All at once it began to snow. A space set apart. I snatched my satchel. We were a small team and we needed help.

The janitor closed for the day. Many years later it began again.

I was alone with the child

Sometimes   her head flopped
sunk   under water   –   I
had to check   was she still
alive   I had   no help
and the next day   did not work
Was this in place of infinity?
Attend to things – indicate politely
an ending   Rescue comes about
and the dog's sharp teeth
set her free

Each shell or barnacle…

Each shell or barnacle

Kingfisher or kite, closely observed. A tarpaulin to rest upon – no sting or carbuncle – leisure caressing all surfaces. No ache (body blithe, unruffled). No significant other, trailing dandelion heads. Pine needles, kelp. Forwards may run forever. The breadth of the breath, the hearth of the heart.

An even temperature. The desire for narrative, the smooth ascent, enclosure the sodden clay. Take a runner nailed into place – a (straight) forward path; an intermittent placing on the doormat.

Playtime pops in – something creative. It is time to engage.

Come side with me

come slide I have
a stake in you the time
has gone extend
your withered arm
there there   Oh me!
Ah you!   yonder yonder
trammel pummel   search
my pockets my inner ear
tell me   what's to do

Prompt

a lone hair a rubber/ed
band a coil of tensile wire
beginning / middle / end
a spool (containing bedlam)
nor did I know how wide
the pigeon's wingspan

My goal

is my entrapment a singular
retribution   my gatepost
my headfirst these flowers
are they not real   their leaves
thin to the touch   pinch one
dig in a nail   prove

Trills

little finger tapping   head
ratcheted to one side
the wind   is changing
a part of you
has stayed   that(a)way

I have folded

my richest care
hung up all ages
a febrile mountain
a spike a thread
to bare

Here in the garden

slightly drops the rain
some of the plants
are intent on survival
the expectant ivy   a sign
of entanglement

I poach my meanings

small forget-me-nots
sideways on   I have something
to give you   I dither bide
my moments   maintain my cult
of never ending   wish my mind
spic and span   a single
token   a saintly sorrow
a pale pink peony
blowsy biddable

Haul

my spectral bag
from cellar to attic – where lays
my past   my crooked mile
– give me a cake   a creel
of marshmallow   throw pence
for my thoughts   a bob
for the metre   sit
at the head   of the table
make true   my room

Here is tin

with nail and clamour
– inverted   unclaimed – give me
a smile   a wooden peg
your helpful hand and I shall reconvene
to an extent: a hill is a scope   a flute
a bower   a glance   a salver   a flume
a tower   small margins
are a mark   of splendour … here is
a seagull   flying away…

All she could see were their eyes
(*Brooklyn*, Colm Toibin)

They flew by   when hers were closed
she still could see   a man
with a bike   taking turns   random
pieces of melon   an ordinary
particular   squint   peep
if you must

Rag bag

torrents of simultaneity:
turgid leaves scales
owl kingfisher
temper   tandem
warm gently to clarify
ringlets ocean   calamine lotion
life's support   mandrake
all in the mud

Rows

of miscellany – a snick
may convey pain   a snicket
deceit   a book may be a stand
on which to place a jar of butter
...the lamps and one of the specks
sent out a tiny gleam...

She looks amongst the stones
her instincts   instruments
of fusion   all
exactly as they were

Words

on a tray (circular
with a small lip) balance
height & breadth:
tents / huts / tenements
some are paupers
→ prickly → dulcet
→ cautionary → plain
some sumptuous
with a curled toe
crumb periwinkle
globule bane

Lark

Folly me dandy
Up from the broad room
Clopped in the cow-pat
Glandular fever
Influence effluence
Safety-pin paraffin
Pickle & candy

Follow me rare
Down for repair
Snapped in the snare
Dip snip & dare
Stock still & stare
Polish & swear
Cauliflower pear

A Causeway Runneling Between Two Lands Either Side of a Parting

Enter, Night Traveller, from the right. Before too long you are sure to encounter some kind of foliage. The dark casts shade over variegation, one cannot trust one's senses & defence is meaningless. 'I have studied the map,' you protest. 'I know well where to place myself, in which direction lies pleasant & fervour, rest & a full stomach. I am Fortunate am I not & bestowed with countenance fair!' (At this point I thinks a smile a grimace).

Such a Strange Land! It is well to be ware, be rid, who knows what straddling behind. Who knows? & half as much again ~ but, I lose track, all folly a head. It is perfectly possible to enter with a difference (stare occasionally at the sun ~ hold for a minute or two for best benefit). I have taken to blessing at random the passers-by ~ why not extend to others for all you wish yourself? Be nice to kindred, vintner, muckler, waif.

Not much ground has been covered yet (you hums to yourself, Traveller, you does ~ I hears you, your little involuntary musings, thinking you's safe). Tralala, tralalee, this is *my* domain. Be merry, go round! This way bastion, that-a-way bludgeon, t'otherway minion, betwixt: true enterprise. Pivot, I tell you! Go for diverse. A pretty picture befalls you, but Lo! What lies under yonder under-leaf, beyond the boundary, aloft? In your trusty pack, I suspect an almanac, a thought for the day, a cross word. 'Who am I to disdain,' you say, 'To chortle from behind a gooseberry bush?' Who am I? Make haste *I* say, you must repose ~ hang up your cummerbund, untether your woebegone, deposit your galoshes by the stump of a tree, light brush & broom; temper & mull, imbibe.

Psst! bonehead ~ time for a tête-à-tête. I have searched for you for days ~ you with the feather/dent/dint in your cap, the piece of a hair, the eyewash & the highbrow, the chosen one. Hounded you say? You have something more to say, you say? Out of sorts? Taken a worse turn? You have been bit? Where is your cloth, your token, your icon, your get one free? Have you booked? You've a nerve of a sort, your sort, bilious as you are (I have added your name to a waiting list – expect a long wait). Sort yourself out! The world is not a shellfish! Call me not a skullduggerer, an anthropoid, a paparazzo, a toothless, gutless ne'er-do-well. Go get your own way!

My words are harsh, but I must to be kind, You Who Would a Traveller Be – you to whom I would give my last hat 'gainst all disaster. All is plagiarism. The water is furring, the air is hardening, a storm is nigh – correct me if I'm wrong. Unbeliever, I am at your service. I intend… my intention is for Hollyhocks to bloom, you to discover & for all the pearls, ingots, doubloons. Wish you a nosegay? All ricochets away & we cannot suspend, much as we try – & I try, O I tries! It behoves me to try. Forgive me… I meant to say… do not turn on a whim, a chafe, a trilobite! Fuel is eating the planet. To go by foot is honourable. When it comes to morrow: Then!

Afterword…

Cento: In my vignettes

I am something   slowly I turn round
tear off   a small shoot   only body
slithering   a painted shadow
collecting itself   We are always
interrupting ourselves   to hide
among the words   My brain locks doors
without   my mind's permission
I catch myself   alone   have had sight
of kindness – a table waiting
so careful   so utterly diligent in detail
I cannot know   what happens next
mad with sanity perfecting silence in my chest
all kinds of ruins   In the day-hours
things are seen as separate   when I'm forgotten
like bits of paper   I am neither near
nor far   it ends behind me in mid-air
I am squat on the porch rug   back
against the bookcase   I turn towards it   face
both ways   &   seem to ask
but still … a person is a path
Who is tearing off this page ?

Source: *Long Poem Magazine* Issue 14

www.ingramcontent.com/pod-product-compliance
Lightning Source LLC
Chambersburg PA
CBHW031636160426
43196CB00006B/446